FIRST PUBLISHED IN 2023
by Amazon KDP Publishing.

Text and illustrations
Copyright © L.Momber 2023.

All rights reserved.

No part of this publication may be reproduced or transmitted in any form, or by any means, electrical, mechanical, photocopying, recording or otherwise without written permission of the publishers.

THE SPOOKTACULAR HALLOWEEN
JOKE BOOK

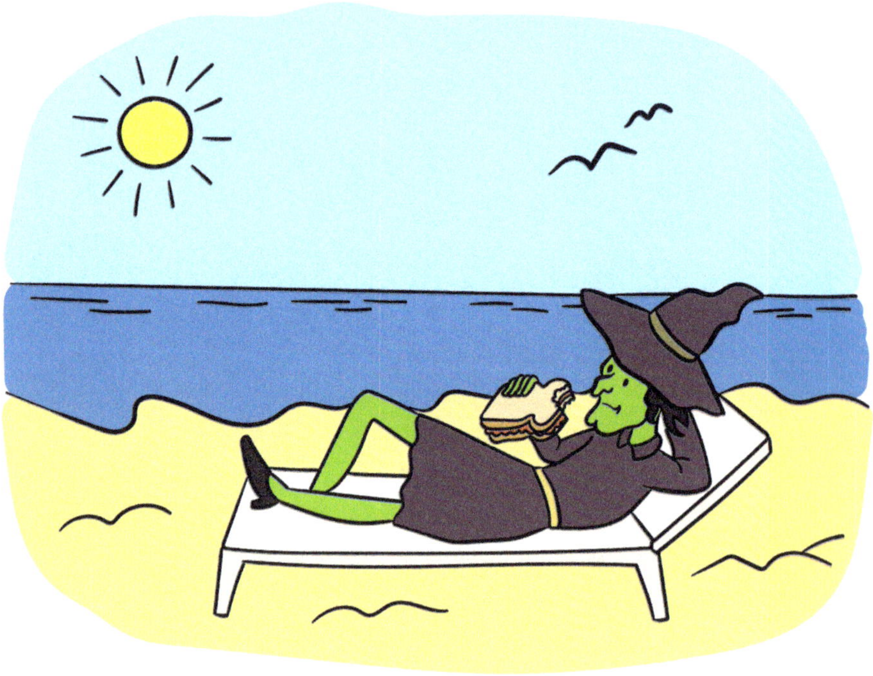

What is a witch's favourite subject at school?

SPELL-ing!

What do you call a witch who lives at the beach?

A SAND-witch!

What did the baby bird say when he knocked on the door for Halloween?

Trick or TWEET!

What does a zombie not need in a house?

A LIVING-room!

What do vampires do with their friends?
FANG-out!

What kind of cars do zombies drive?
MONSTER trucks!

Why are vampires easily fooled?
Because they're SUCKERS!

Who did the little monster ask for when he was scared?
His MUMMY!

What did the Mummy say to her child?
Go and clean your TOMB!

What does a panda ghost eat?
Bam-BOO!

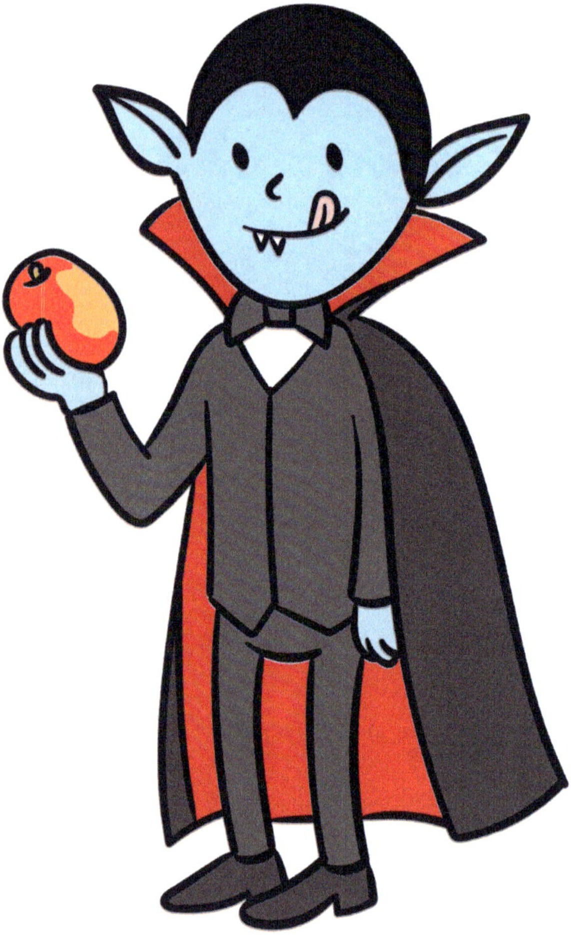

What is a vampire's favourite fruit?
A NECK-tarine!

What is a ghost's favourite game?
Hide and SHRIEK!

Why are skeletons so calm?
Beacuse nothing gets UNDER THEIR SKIN!

What do ghosts use to clean their hair?
Sham-BOO!

Why was the mummy scared to take a vacation?
He didn't want to UNWIND!

Why are vampires bad at art?
Because they are only able to DRAW BLOOD!

Why did the ghost quit studying?
Because he was too GHOUL for school!

Where do Zombies live?
On a DEAD-end street!

How do ghosts send letters?
Through the GHOST-office!

When do cows turn into werewolves?
During a full MOOOOOOn!

What do ghosts wear when they have blurry vision?

SPOOK-tacles!

Why is Dracula so unpopular?

Because he's a PAIN IN THE NECK!

Where do witches go to look up random facts?
WICCA-pedia!

Where does a skeleton go for a fun night?
Anywhere, as long as it's a HIP-JOINT!

Why can't vampires go to a barbecue?
Because they're afraid of STAKES!

What is a ghost's favorite day of the week?
FRIGHT-day!

What do you call a nervous witch?
A TWITCH!

Do mummies prefer white or brown bread?
Neither, they prefer a WRAP!

What do kids today like more than halloween candy?
Hallo-MEMES!

What is a skeleton's favorite song?
"Bad to the BONE!"

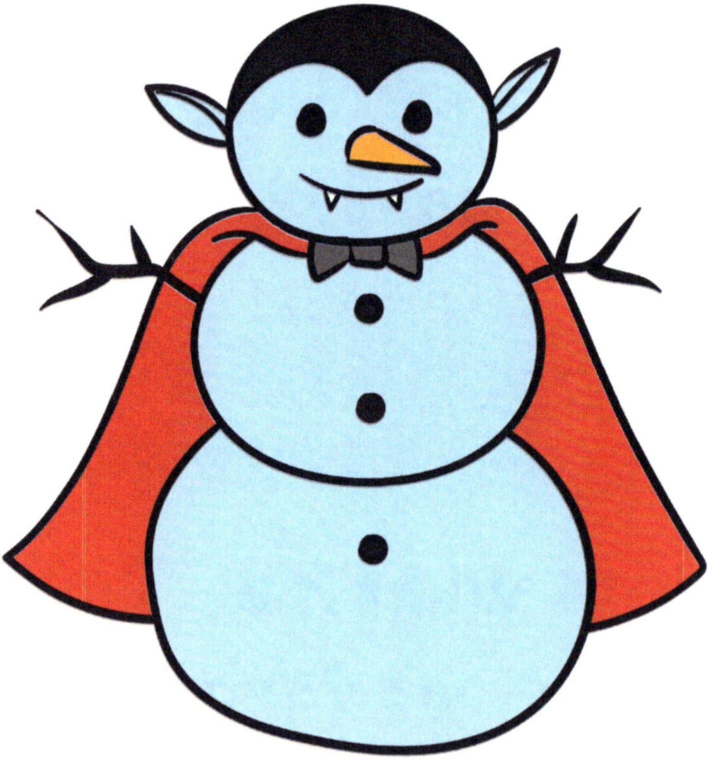

What do you get when you cross a vampire and a snowman?
FROSTBITE!

Why do mummies have trouble keeping friends?
Because they're too WRAPPED-up in themselves!

What's the best way to punish a teenage monster?
Limit their SCREAM-time!

Why did the vampire read a newspaper?
Because he heard it had great CIRCULATION!

Which key opens a haunted house?
A SPOOK-key!

Why did Dracula take cold medicine?
Because he was COFFIN too much!

What do you call a monster who tells great halloween jokes?
A PUN-king!

What is a monster's favourite desert?
Ice-SCREAM!

How does the devil get people to sell their souls??

By using SIN-fluencer marketing!

What is a skeleton's favorite instrument?

A trom-BONE!

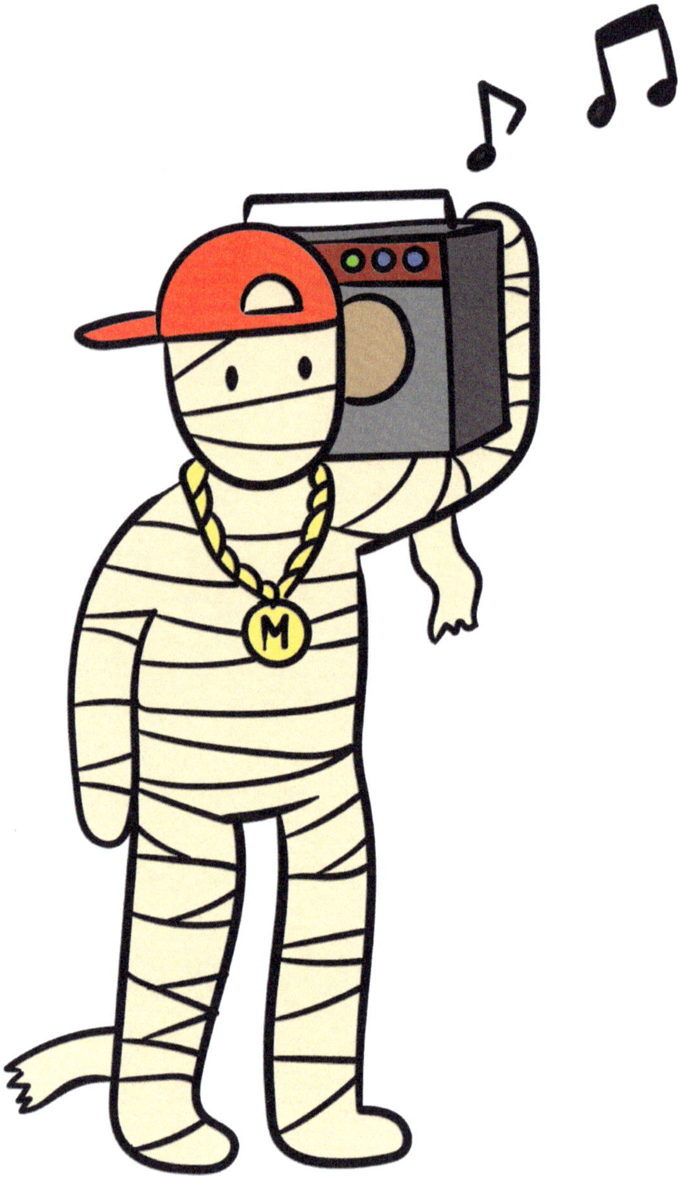
M

What is a ghoul's favourite drink flavour?
Lemon and SLIME!

What is a mummie's favourite type of music?
WRAP-music!

Why was the witch suspicious of the ghost?
Because she could see right-THROUGH him!

What's the problem with twin witches?
You never know which WITCH is which!

How did the skeleton know it was going to rain on halloween?
He could feel it in his BONES!

What is a monster's favourite food?
GHOUL-ash!

Why don't ghosts like the rain?
Because it dampens their SPIRITS!

Why do mummies never reveal their true age?
Because they like to keep it under WRAPS!

What kind of snack did the tarantula get at the fun fair?
Corn on the COB-WEB!

Why does a witch ride a broomstick?
So she can make a clean- GETAWAY!

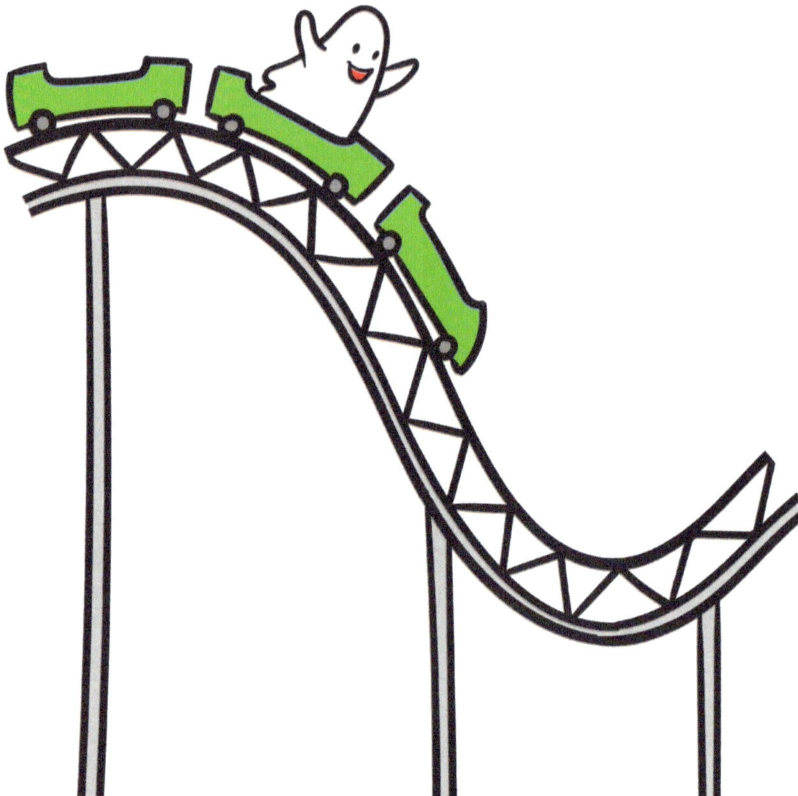

What is a ghost's favourite ride at the fun fair?
The Roller-GHOSTER!

Why can't skeletons play church music?
Because they have no-ORGANS!

How do vampires get around on halloween?
They use blood-VESSELS!

What did one ghost say to the other ghost?
GET A LIFE!

Knock knock. Who's there?
BOO. Boo who?
DON'T CRY. It's only halloween!

What happened to the devil's You Tube channel?
It got DEMON-itised!

What is a Scottish zombie's favorite Shakespeare play?
McDEATH!

What did the ghost say to his therapist?
I used to be some-BODY!

What is a ghost's favourite sandwich spread?
SCREAM-cheese!

What did the pumpkin say to the pumpkin carver?
CUT IT OUT!

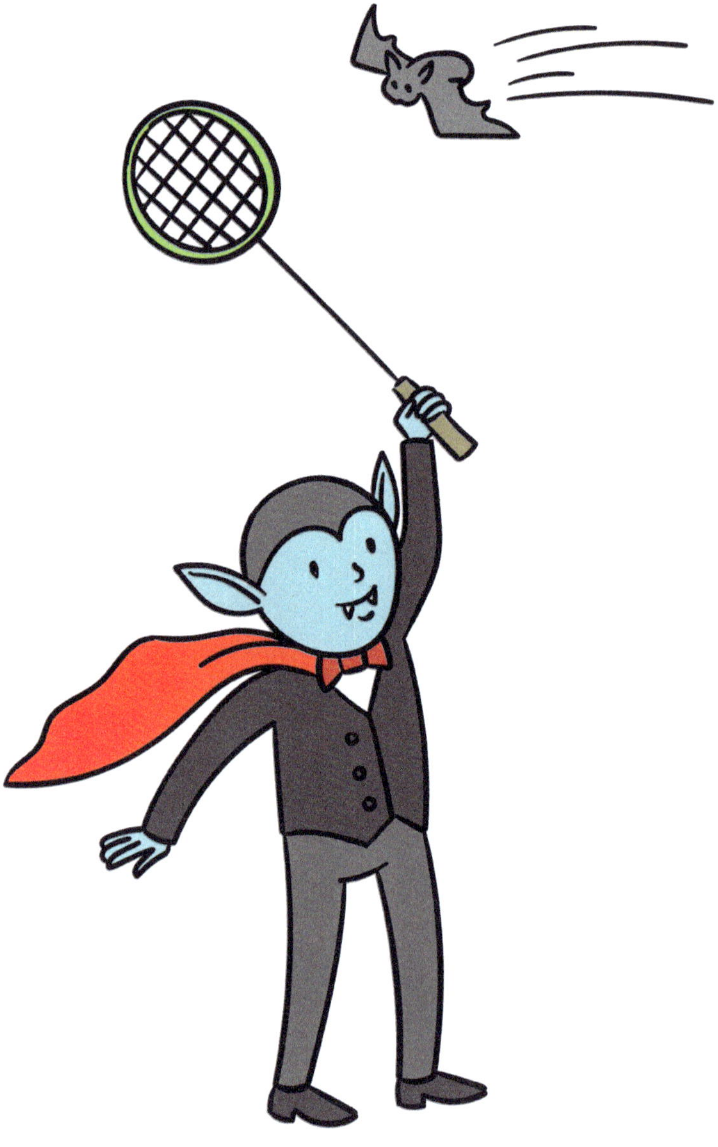

How does a witch tell the time?
With a WITCH-watch!

What's a vampire's favourite sport?
BAT-minton!

What happened to the guy who couldn't keep up payments to the exorcist?
He was re-POSSESSED!

What do you call a chicken ghost?
A POULTRY-geist!

How do you make a witch stew?
Keep her waiting for HOURS!

Who won the skeleton beauty contest?
No-BODY!

Where do mummies go for a swim?
The DEAD sea!

What do you call two witches who live together?
BROOM-mates!

What did the vampire say to his assistant?
FANGS for your help!

What is a monster's favourite play?
Romeo and GHOUL-iet!

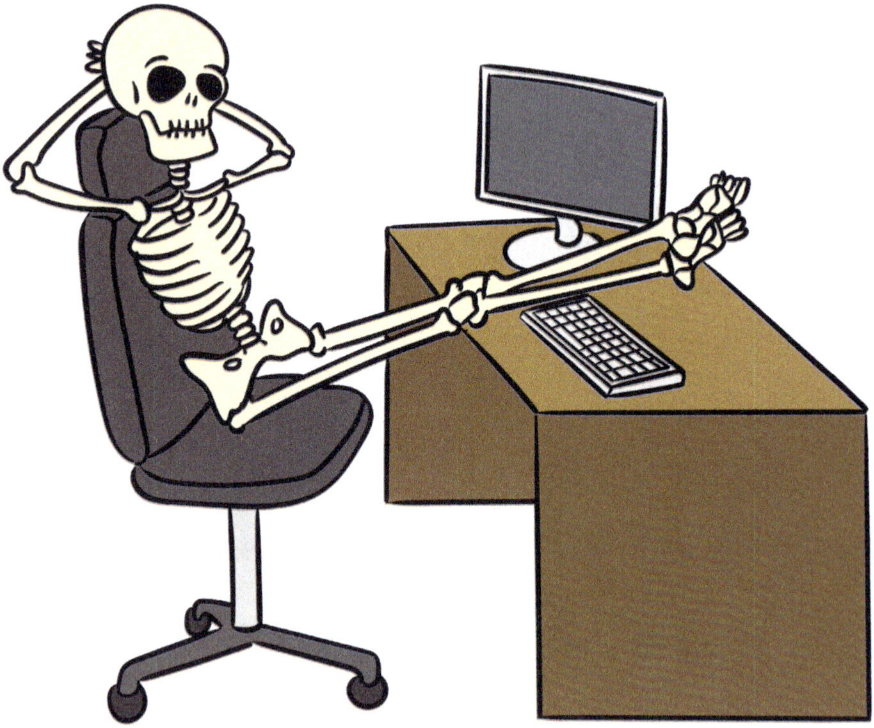

Where do skeletons invest their money?
In the CRYPT-O market!

What do you call a skeleton who won't work?
Lazy-BONES!

Why did the Headless Horseman get a job?

He was trying to get a-HEAD in life!

Why did the ghost quit his job?

Because they kept making him work the GRAVEYARD-shift!

Why do vampires need mouth wash?
Because they have BAT-breath!

What is a skeleton's favourite food?
Spare-RIBS!

What is a vampire's favourite holiday?
FANGS-giving!

What is a zombie's favourute breakfast cereal?
Rice-CREEPIES!

What do skeletons fly around in?
A SKELE-COPTER!

What did the fisherman say on halloween?
Trick or TROUT!

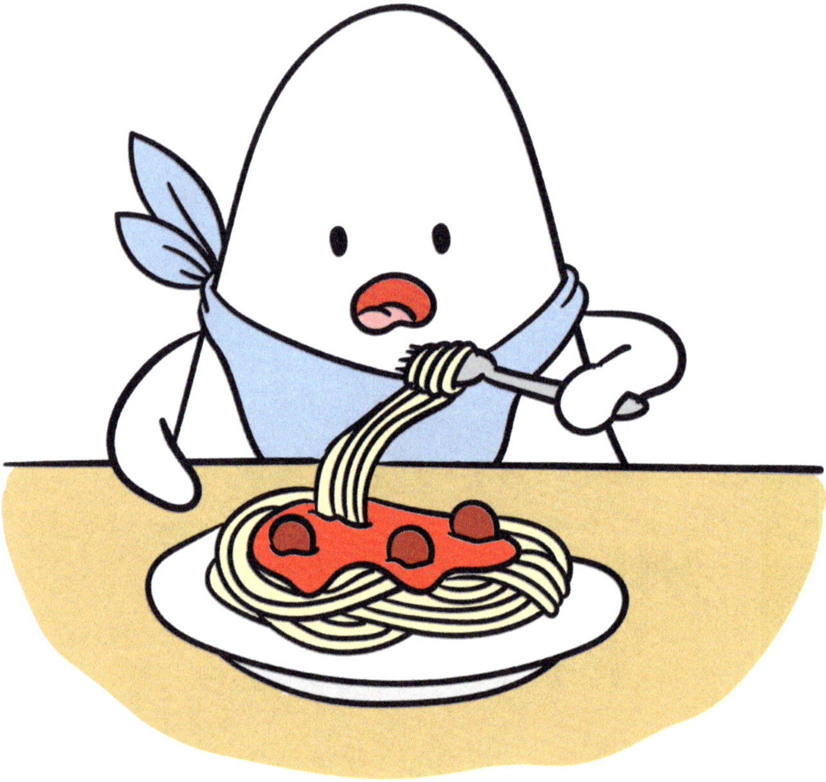

What did the ghost eat for dinner?
SPOOK-ghetti!

Why don't witches ride their brooms when they're angry?
Because they might fly off the HANDLE!

How does a vampire enter his house?
Through the BAT-flap!

Where does Dracula keep his money?
In a BLOOD-bank!

How do monsters tell their future?
They read their HORROR-SCOPE!

What did one skeleton say to the other?
I've got a BONE to pick with you!

Knock knock. Who's there? Ivana. Ivana who?
IVANA suck your blood!

What did Dracula say about his wife?
It was love at first-BITE!

What does a ghoul put on its pizza?
MONSTER-ella cheese!

Why do ghosts like end of season sales?
Because they are bargain-HAUNTERS!

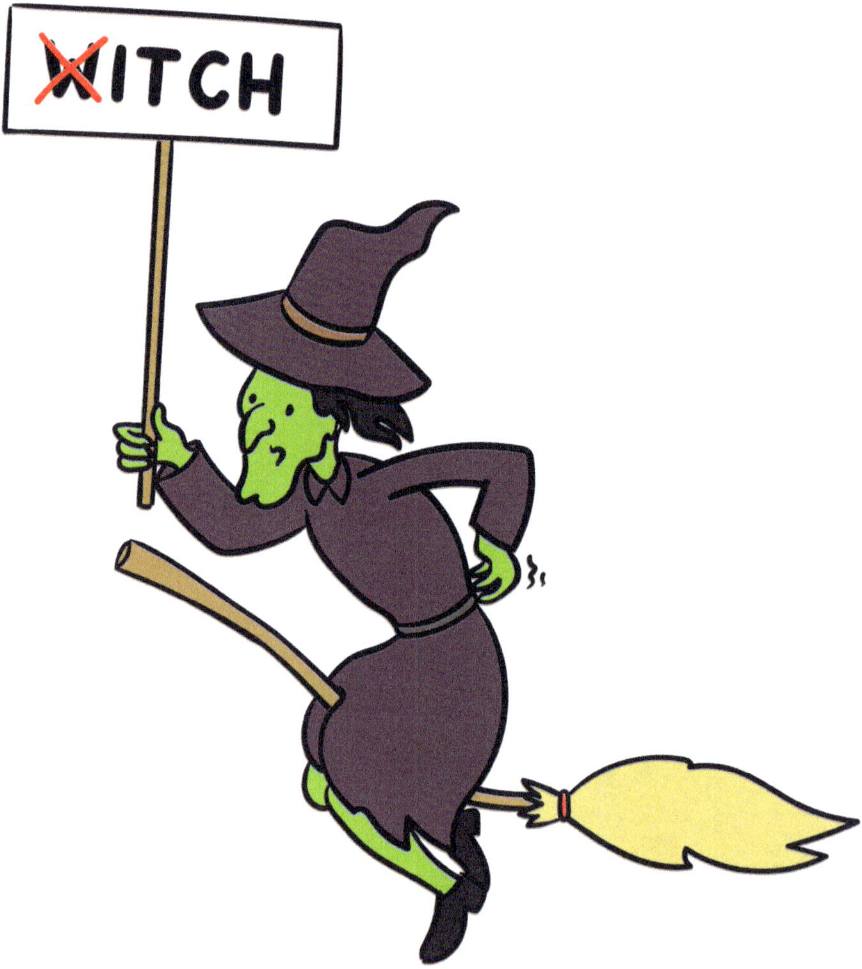
~~W~~ITCH

What did the skeleton say before eating dinner?
BONE-appétit!

How do you make a witch itch?
Take away the "W"!

What kind of horses do ghosts ride?
NIGHT-mares!

Knock knock! Who's there? Justin! Justin who?
JUSTIN-time for Halloween!

What do you call two recently married spiders?

Newly-WEBS!

What do ghosts eat for lunch?

BOO-rritos!

Why did the skeleton
go to the party alone?
Beacause he had
no-BODY to go with!

What kind of make-up
do ghosts wear?
Ma-SCARE-a!

What do witch's use to style their hair?
SCARE-spray!

When do zombies finish trick or treating?
When they are DEAD-tired!

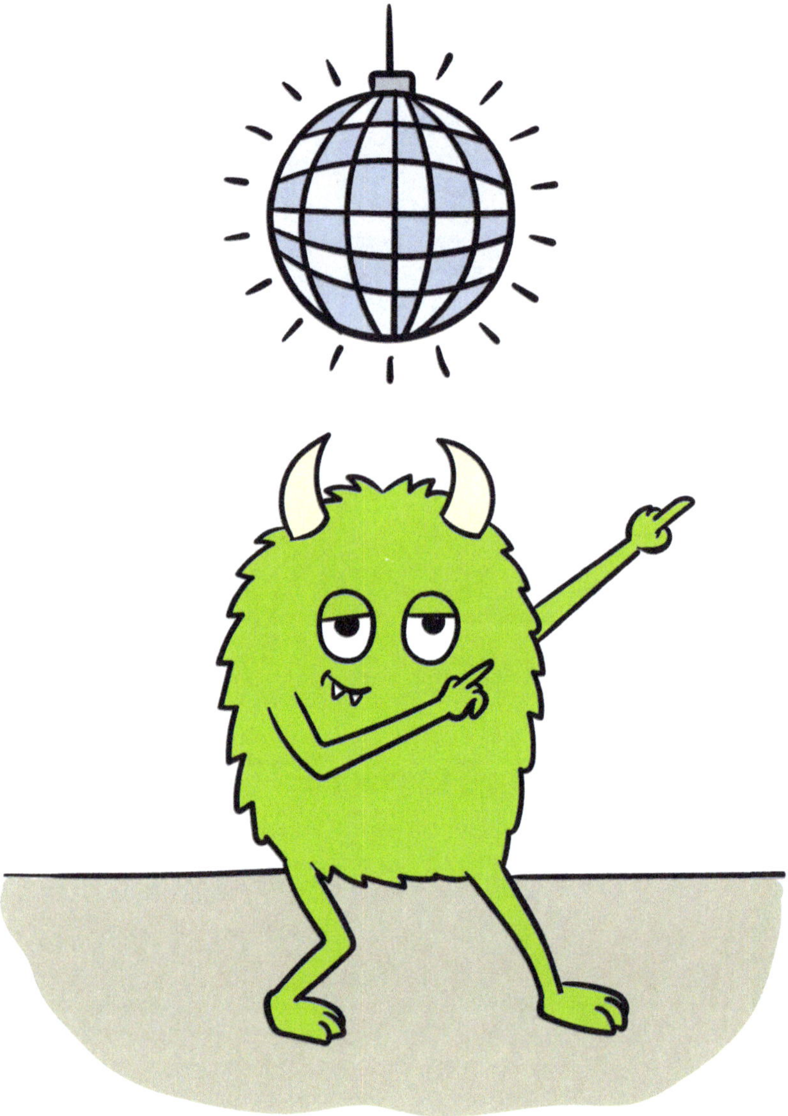

How do mummies begin writing a letter?
TOMB-whom it may concern!

What kind of monster loves to go to a disco?
The BOOGIE-man!

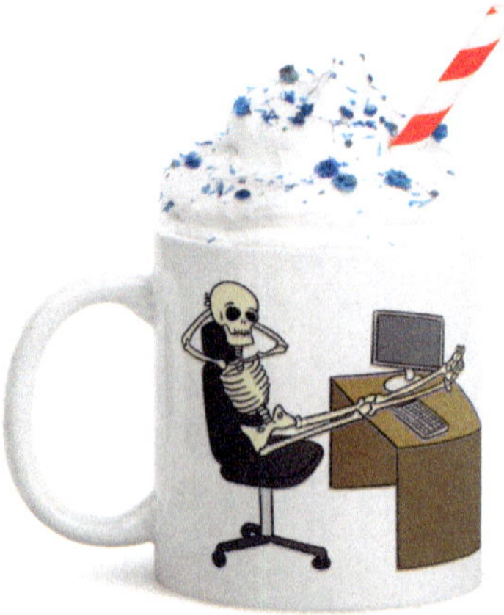

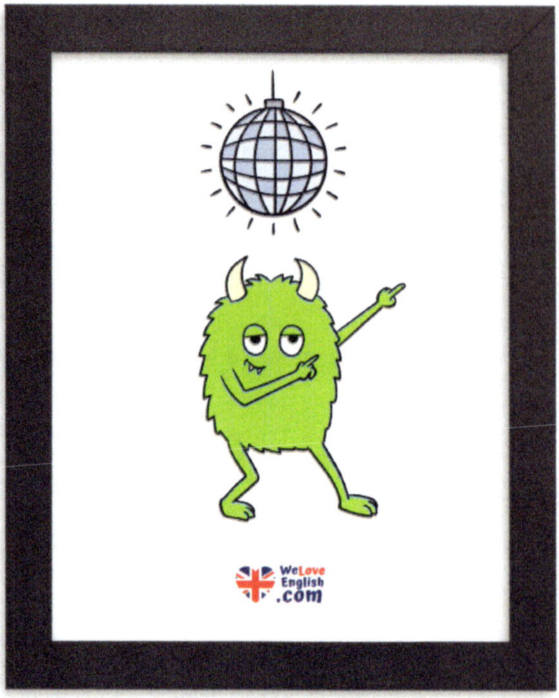
WeLove
English
.com

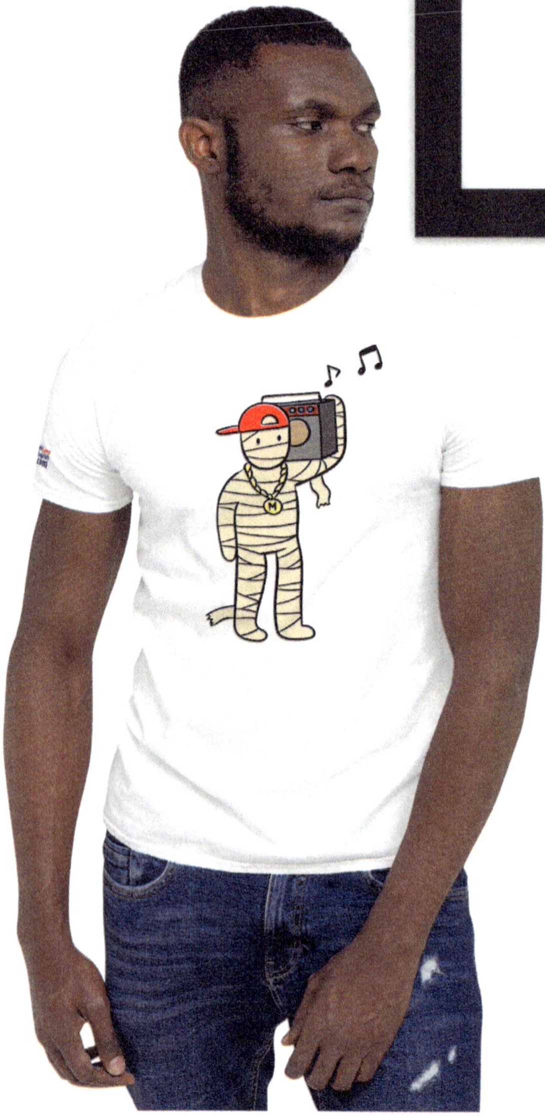

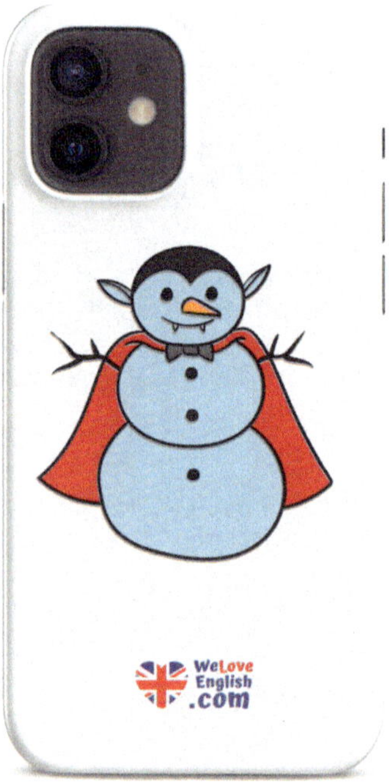
WeLove
English
.com

VISIT OUR SHOP!

Scan the QR code or visit
weloveenglish.com

Perfect gifts for young AND older English Language Fans!

LAUGH AND LEARN!